THE *budget* PLANNER

NAME: _____

PHONE: _____

EMAIL: _____

ANNUAL SUMMARY

Yearly Figures

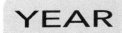
YEAR

Budgeted
Income : _____
Expenses: _____
Saving: _____
Emergency Fund: _____
Debt Repayment: _____

Actual
Income : _____
Expenses: _____
Saving: _____
Emergency Fund: _____
Debt Repayment: _____

JANUARY
Income : _____
Expenses: _____
Saving: _____
Emergency Fund: _____
Debt Repayment: _____

FEBRUARY
Income : _____
Expenses: _____
Saving: _____
Emergency Fund: _____
Debt Repayment: _____

MARCH
Income : _____
Expenses: _____
Saving: _____
Emergency Fund: _____
Debt Repayment: _____

APRIL
Income : _____
Expenses: _____
Saving: _____
Emergency Fund: _____
Debt Repayment: _____

MAY
Income : _____
Expenses: _____
Saving: _____
Emergency Fund: _____
Debt Repayment: _____

JUNE
Income : _____
Expenses: _____
Saving: _____
Emergency Fund: _____
Debt Repayment: _____

JULY
Income : _____
Expenses: _____
Saving: _____
Emergency Fund: _____
Debt Repayment: _____

AUGUST
Income : _____
Expenses: _____
Saving: _____
Emergency Fund: _____
Debt Repayment: _____

SEPTEMBER
Income : _____
Expenses: _____
Saving: _____
Emergency Fund: _____
Debt Repayment: _____

OCTOBER
Income : _____
Expenses: _____
Saving: _____
Emergency Fund: _____
Debt Repayment: _____

NOVEMBER
Income : _____
Expenses: _____
Saving: _____
Emergency Fund: _____
Debt Repayment: _____

DECEMBER
Income : _____
Expenses: _____
Saving: _____
Emergency Fund: _____
Debt Repayment: _____

ANNUAL EXPENSES

JANUARY
Expense	Cost	Date Due
_____	_____	__/__/__
_____	_____	__/__/__
_____	_____	__/__/__
_____	_____	__/__/__
_____	_____	__/__/__
_____	_____	__/__/__
_____	_____	__/__/__

FEBRUARY
Expense	Cost	Date Due
_____	_____	__/__/__
_____	_____	__/__/__
_____	_____	__/__/__
_____	_____	__/__/__
_____	_____	__/__/__
_____	_____	__/__/__
_____	_____	__/__/__

MARCH
Expense	Cost	Date Due
_____	_____	__/__/__
_____	_____	__/__/__
_____	_____	__/__/__
_____	_____	__/__/__
_____	_____	__/__/__
_____	_____	__/__/__
_____	_____	__/__/__

APRIL
Expense	Cost	Date Due
_____	_____	__/__/__
_____	_____	__/__/__
_____	_____	__/__/__
_____	_____	__/__/__
_____	_____	__/__/__
_____	_____	__/__/__
_____	_____	__/__/__

MAY
Expense	Cost	Date Due
_____	_____	__/__/__
_____	_____	__/__/__
_____	_____	__/__/__
_____	_____	__/__/__
_____	_____	__/__/__
_____	_____	__/__/__
_____	_____	__/__/__

JUNE
Expense	Cost	Date Due
_____	_____	__/__/__
_____	_____	__/__/__
_____	_____	__/__/__
_____	_____	__/__/__
_____	_____	__/__/__
_____	_____	__/__/__
_____	_____	__/__/__

JULY
Expense	Cost	Date Due
_____	_____	__/__/__
_____	_____	__/__/__
_____	_____	__/__/__
_____	_____	__/__/__
_____	_____	__/__/__
_____	_____	__/__/__
_____	_____	__/__/__

AUGUST
Expense	Cost	Date Due
_____	_____	__/__/__
_____	_____	__/__/__
_____	_____	__/__/__
_____	_____	__/__/__
_____	_____	__/__/__
_____	_____	__/__/__
_____	_____	__/__/__

SEPTEMBER
Expense	Cost	Date Due
_____	_____	__/__/__
_____	_____	__/__/__
_____	_____	__/__/__
_____	_____	__/__/__
_____	_____	__/__/__
_____	_____	__/__/__
_____	_____	__/__/__

OCTOBER
Expense	Cost	Date Due
_____	_____	__/__/__
_____	_____	__/__/__
_____	_____	__/__/__
_____	_____	__/__/__
_____	_____	__/__/__
_____	_____	__/__/__
_____	_____	__/__/__

NOVEMBER
Expense	Cost	Date Due
_____	_____	__/__/__
_____	_____	__/__/__
_____	_____	__/__/__
_____	_____	__/__/__
_____	_____	__/__/__
_____	_____	__/__/__
_____	_____	__/__/__

DECEMBER
Expense	Cost	Date Due
_____	_____	__/__/__
_____	_____	__/__/__
_____	_____	__/__/__
_____	_____	__/__/__
_____	_____	__/__/__
_____	_____	__/__/__
_____	_____	__/__/__

Bank *Account* Details

DESCRIPTION:	**DESCRIPTION:**
ACCOUNT #:	ACCOUNT #:
ROUTING #:	ROUTING #:
BANK NAME:	BANK NAME:
PHONE #:	PHONE #:
ADDRESS:	ADDRESS:
WEBSITE:	WEBSITE:
USERNAME:	USERNAME:
PASSWORD:	PASSWORD:
DEBIT / CC #:	DEBIT / CC #:
PIN:	PIN:
DEBIT / CC #:	DEBIT / CC #:
PIN:	PIN:
NOTES:	NOTES:
DESCRIPTION:	**DESCRIPTION:**
ACCOUNT #:	ACCOUNT #:
ROUTING #:	ROUTING #:
BANK NAME:	BANK NAME:
PHONE #:	PHONE #:
ADDRESS:	ADDRESS:
WEBSITE:	WEBSITE:
USERNAME:	USERNAME:
PASSWORD:	PASSWORD:
DEBIT / CC #:	DEBIT / CC #:
PIN:	PIN:
DEBIT / CC #:	DEBIT / CC #:
PIN:	PIN:
NOTES:	NOTES:

Bank *Account* Details

DESCRIPTION:

ACCOUNT #:
ROUTING #:
BANK NAME:
PHONE #:
ADDRESS:

WEBSITE:
USERNAME:
PASSWORD:
DEBIT / CC #:
PIN:
DEBIT / CC #:
PIN:
NOTES:

DESCRIPTION:

ACCOUNT #:
ROUTING #:
BANK NAME:
PHONE #:
ADDRESS:

WEBSITE:
USERNAME:
PASSWORD:
DEBIT / CC #:
PIN:
DEBIT / CC #:
PIN:
NOTES:

DESCRIPTION:

ACCOUNT #:
ROUTING #:
BANK NAME:
PHONE #:
ADDRESS:

WEBSITE:
USERNAME:
PASSWORD:
DEBIT / CC #:
PIN:
DEBIT / CC #:
PIN:
NOTES:

DESCRIPTION:

ACCOUNT #:
ROUTING #:
BANK NAME:
PHONE #:
ADDRESS:

WEBSITE:
USERNAME:
PASSWORD:
DEBIT / CC #:
PIN:
DEBIT / CC #:
PIN:
NOTES:

Bill Tracker

BILL TO BE PAID	DATE	JAN	FEB	MAR	APR	MAY	JUN	JUL	AUG	SEP	OCT	NOV	DEC

TOTAL EXPENSES

MONTHLY DONATION TRACKER

Budget _____

JANUARY

Date	Charity	Reg. No.	Amount	Notes	Tax
TOTAL					

FEBRUARY

Date	Charity	Reg. No.	Amount	Notes	Tax
TOTAL					

MARCH

Date	Charity	Reg. No.	Amount	Notes	Tax
TOTAL					

APRIL

Date	Charity	Reg. No.	Amount	Notes	Tax
TOTAL					

MAY

Date	Charity	Reg. No.	Amount	Notes	Tax
TOTAL					

JUNE

Date	Charity	Reg. No.	Amount	Notes	Tax
TOTAL					

JULY

Date	Charity	Reg. No.	Amount	Notes	Tax
TOTAL					

AUGUST

Date	Charity	Reg. No.	Amount	Notes	Tax
TOTAL					

SEPTEMBER

Date	Charity	Reg. No.	Amount	Notes	Tax
TOTAL					

OCTOBER

Date	Charity	Reg. No.	Amount	Notes	Tax
TOTAL					

NOVEMBER

Date	Charity	Reg. No.	Amount	Notes	Tax
TOTAL					

DECEMBER

Date	Charity	Reg. No.	Amount	Notes	Tax
TOTAL					

TOTAL _____

THE *Debt* TRACKER

ACCOUNT:

MINIMUM: _____ DUE DATE: _____

CREDIT LIMIT: _____ INTEREST RATE: _____

ACCOUNT ID: _____ PASSWORD: _____

BALANCE	PAYMENT	DATE	NEW BALANCE

THE *Debt* TRACKER

ACCOUNT:

MINIMUM: _____ DUE DATE: _____

CREDIT LIMIT: _____ INTEREST RATE: _____

ACCOUNT ID _____ PASSWORD: _____

BALANCE	PAYMENT	DATE	NEW BALANCE

THE *Savings* TRACKER

SAVING FOR: GOAL:

DATE	DEPOSIT	BALANCE	DATE	DEPOSIT	BALANCE

THE *Savings* TRACKER

SAVING FOR: GOAL:

DATE	DEPOSIT	BALANCE	DATE	DEPOSIT	BALANCE

Monthly Budget Worksheet

Month : _____   Year : _____

INCOME

Income 1	Income 2
Other Income	Total Income

SAVINGS

Starting Balance _____
Ending Balance _____

DEBT

Starting Balance _____
Ending Balance _____

DUE DATE	PAID	WHICH BILL	BUDGET	SPENT
		TOTAL		

GOALS

BY WHEN?	SAVING FOR WHAT?	MONTHLY GOAL	TOTAL NEEDED

ACTUALLY SAVED: _____
AMOUNT LEFT GOAL: _____

BY WHEN?	SAVING FOR WHAT?	MONTHLY GOAL	TOTAL NEEDED

ACTUALLY SAVED: _____
AMOUNT LEFT GOAL: _____

BY WHEN?	SAVING FOR WHAT?	MONTHLY GOAL	TOTAL NEEDED

ACTUALLY SAVED: _____
AMOUNT LEFT GOAL: _____

NOTES:

Daily EXPENSE TRACKER

DATE	DESCRIPTION	CATEGORY	AMOUNT	CASH	CREDIT	DEBIT	NEED	WANT

TOTAL EXPENSES

Daily EXPENSE TRACKER

DATE	DESCRIPTION	CATEGORY	AMOUNT	CASH	CREDIT	DEBIT	NEED	WANT

TOTAL EXPENSES

Daily EXPENSE TRACKER

DATE	DESCRIPTION	CATEGORY	AMOUNT	CASH	CREDIT	DEBIT	NEED	WANT

TOTAL EXPENSES

Monthly Budget Worksheet

Month: _____ Year: _____

INCOME

Income 1	Income 2
Other Income	Total Income

SAVINGS

Starting Balance _____

Ending Balance _____

DEBT

Starting Balance _____

Ending Balance _____

DUE DATE	PAID	WHICH BILL	BUDGET	SPENT
		TOTAL		

GOALS

BY WHEN?	SAVING FOR WHAT?	MONTHLY GOAL	TOTAL NEEDED

ACTUALLY SAVED: _____

AMOUNT LEFT GOAL: _____

BY WHEN?	SAVING FOR WHAT?	MONTHLY GOAL	TOTAL NEEDED

ACTUALLY SAVED: _____

AMOUNT LEFT GOAL: _____

BY WHEN?	SAVING FOR WHAT?	MONTHLY GOAL	TOTAL NEEDED

ACTUALLY SAVED: _____

AMOUNT LEFT GOAL: _____

NOTES:

Daily EXPENSE TRACKER

DATE	DESCRIPTION	CATEGORY	AMOUNT	CASH	CREDIT	DEBIT	NEED	WANT

TOTAL EXPENSES

Daily EXPENSE TRACKER

DATE	DESCRIPTION	CATEGORY	AMOUNT	CASH	CREDIT	DEBIT	NEED	WANT

TOTAL EXPENSES

Daily EXPENSE TRACKER

DATE	DESCRIPTION	CATEGORY	AMOUNT	CASH	CREDIT	DEBIT	NEED	WANT

TOTAL EXPENSES

Monthly Budget Worksheet

Month : _____ Year : _____

INCOME

| Income 1 | Income 2 |
| Other Income | Total Income |

SAVINGS

Starting Balance _____
Ending Balance _____

DEBT

Starting Balance _____
Ending Balance _____

DUE DATE	PAID	WHICH BILL	BUDGET	SPENT
		TOTAL		

GOALS

BY WHEN?	SAVING FOR WHAT?	MONTHLY GOAL	TOTAL NEEDED

ACTUALLY SAVED: _____
AMOUNT LEFT GOAL: _____

BY WHEN?	SAVING FOR WHAT?	MONTHLY GOAL	TOTAL NEEDED

ACTUALLY SAVED: _____
AMOUNT LEFT GOAL: _____

BY WHEN?	SAVING FOR WHAT?	MONTHLY GOAL	TOTAL NEEDED

ACTUALLY SAVED: _____
AMOUNT LEFT GOAL: _____

NOTES:

Daily EXPENSE TRACKER

DATE	DESCRIPTION	CATEGORY	AMOUNT	CASH	CREDIT	DEBIT	NEED	WANT

TOTAL EXPENSES

Daily EXPENSE TRACKER

DATE	DESCRIPTION	CATEGORY	AMOUNT	CASH	CREDIT	DEBIT	NEED	WANT

TOTAL EXPENSES

Daily EXPENSE TRACKER

DATE	DESCRIPTION	CATEGORY	AMOUNT	CASH	CREDIT	DEBIT	NEED	WANT

TOTAL EXPENSES

Monthly Budget Worksheet

Month: _____   Year: _____

INCOME

Income 1	Income 2
Other Income	Total Income

SAVINGS

Starting Balance _____
Ending Balance _____

DEBT

Starting Balance _____
Ending Balance _____

DUE DATE	PAID	WHICH BILL	BUDGET	SPENT
		TOTAL		

GOALS

BY WHEN?	SAVING FOR WHAT?	MONTHLY GOAL	TOTAL NEEDED

ACTUALLY SAVED: _____
AMOUNT LEFT GOAL: _____

BY WHEN?	SAVING FOR WHAT?	MONTHLY GOAL	TOTAL NEEDED

ACTUALLY SAVED: _____
AMOUNT LEFT GOAL: _____

BY WHEN?	SAVING FOR WHAT?	MONTHLY GOAL	TOTAL NEEDED

ACTUALLY SAVED: _____
AMOUNT LEFT GOAL: _____

NOTES:

Daily EXPENSE TRACKER

DATE	DESCRIPTION	CATEGORY	AMOUNT	CASH	CREDIT	DEBIT	NEED	WANT

TOTAL EXPENSES

Daily EXPENSE TRACKER

DATE	DESCRIPTION	CATEGORY	AMOUNT	CASH	CREDIT	DEBIT	NEED	WANT

TOTAL EXPENSES

Daily EXPENSE TRACKER

DATE	DESCRIPTION	CATEGORY	AMOUNT	CASH	CREDIT	DEBIT	NEED	WANT

TOTAL EXPENSES

Monthly Budget Worksheet

Month : _____ Year : _____

INCOME

Income 1	Income 2
Other Income	Total Income

SAVINGS

Starting Balance _____

Ending Balance _____

DEBT

Starting Balance _____

Ending Balance _____

DUE DATE	PAID	WHICH BILL	BUDGET	SPENT
		TOTAL		

GOALS

BY WHEN?	SAVING FOR WHAT?	MONTHLY GOAL	TOTAL NEEDED

ACTUALLY SAVED: _____

AMOUNT LEFT GOAL: _____

BY WHEN?	SAVING FOR WHAT?	MONTHLY GOAL	TOTAL NEEDED

ACTUALLY SAVED: _____

AMOUNT LEFT GOAL: _____

BY WHEN?	SAVING FOR WHAT?	MONTHLY GOAL	TOTAL NEEDED

ACTUALLY SAVED: _____

AMOUNT LEFT GOAL: _____

NOTES:

Daily EXPENSE TRACKER

DATE	DESCRIPTION	CATEGORY	AMOUNT	CASH	CREDIT	DEBIT	NEED	WANT

TOTAL EXPENSES

Daily EXPENSE TRACKER

DATE	DESCRIPTION	CATEGORY	AMOUNT	CASH	CREDIT	DEBIT	NEED	WANT

TOTAL EXPENSES

Daily EXPENSE TRACKER

DATE	DESCRIPTION	CATEGORY	AMOUNT	CASH	CREDIT	DEBIT	NEED	WANT

TOTAL EXPENSES

Monthly Budget Worksheet

Month : _____ Year : _____

INCOME

- Income 1
- Income 2
- Other Income
- Total Income

SAVINGS

Starting Balance _____
Ending Balance _____

DEBT

Starting Balance _____
Ending Balance _____

DUE DATE	PAID	WHICH BILL	BUDGET	SPENT
		TOTAL		

GOALS

BY WHEN?	SAVING FOR WHAT?	MONTHLY GOAL	TOTAL NEEDED

ACTUALLY SAVED: _____
AMOUNT LEFT GOAL: _____

BY WHEN?	SAVING FOR WHAT?	MONTHLY GOAL	TOTAL NEEDED

ACTUALLY SAVED: _____
AMOUNT LEFT GOAL: _____

BY WHEN?	SAVING FOR WHAT?	MONTHLY GOAL	TOTAL NEEDED

ACTUALLY SAVED: _____
AMOUNT LEFT GOAL: _____

NOTES:

Daily EXPENSE TRACKER

DATE	DESCRIPTION	CATEGORY	AMOUNT	CASH	CREDIT	DEBIT	NEED	WANT

TOTAL EXPENSES

Daily EXPENSE TRACKER

DATE	DESCRIPTION	CATEGORY	AMOUNT	CASH	CREDIT	DEBIT	NEED	WANT

TOTAL EXPENSES

Daily EXPENSE TRACKER

DATE	DESCRIPTION	CATEGORY	AMOUNT	CASH	CREDIT	DEBIT	NEED	WANT

TOTAL EXPENSES

Monthly Budget Worksheet

Month: _____   Year: _____

INCOME

Income 1	Income 2
Other Income	Total Income

SAVINGS

Starting Balance _____
Ending Balance _____

DEBT

Starting Balance _____
Ending Balance _____

DUE DATE	PAID	WHICH BILL	BUDGET	SPENT
		TOTAL		

GOALS

BY WHEN?	SAVING FOR WHAT?	MONTHLY GOAL	TOTAL NEEDED

ACTUALLY SAVED: _____
AMOUNT LEFT GOAL: _____

BY WHEN?	SAVING FOR WHAT?	MONTHLY GOAL	TOTAL NEEDED

ACTUALLY SAVED: _____
AMOUNT LEFT GOAL: _____

BY WHEN?	SAVING FOR WHAT?	MONTHLY GOAL	TOTAL NEEDED

ACTUALLY SAVED: _____
AMOUNT LEFT GOAL: _____

NOTES:

Daily EXPENSE TRACKER

DATE	DESCRIPTION	CATEGORY	AMOUNT	CASH	CREDIT	DEBIT	NEED	WANT

TOTAL EXPENSES

Daily EXPENSE TRACKER

DATE	DESCRIPTION	CATEGORY	AMOUNT	CASH	CREDIT	DEBIT	NEED	WANT

TOTAL EXPENSES

Daily EXPENSE TRACKER

DATE	DESCRIPTION	CATEGORY	AMOUNT	CASH	CREDIT	DEBIT	NEED	WANT

TOTAL EXPENSES

Monthly Budget Worksheet

Month : _____   Year : _____

INCOME

Income 1	Income 2
Other Income	Total Income

SAVINGS

Starting Balance _____

Ending Balance _____

DEBT

Starting Balance _____

Ending Balance _____

DUE DATE	PAID	WHICH BILL	BUDGET	SPENT
		TOTAL		

GOALS

BY WHEN?	SAVING FOR WHAT?	MONTHLY GOAL	TOTAL NEEDED

ACTUALLY SAVED: _____

AMOUNT LEFT GOAL: _____

BY WHEN?	SAVING FOR WHAT?	MONTHLY GOAL	TOTAL NEEDED

ACTUALLY SAVED: _____

AMOUNT LEFT GOAL: _____

BY WHEN?	SAVING FOR WHAT?	MONTHLY GOAL	TOTAL NEEDED

ACTUALLY SAVED: _____

AMOUNT LEFT GOAL: _____

NOTES:

Daily EXPENSE TRACKER

DATE	DESCRIPTION	CATEGORY	AMOUNT	CASH	CREDIT	DEBIT	NEED	WANT

TOTAL EXPENSES

Daily EXPENSE TRACKER

DATE	DESCRIPTION	CATEGORY	AMOUNT	CASH	CREDIT	DEBIT	NEED	WANT

TOTAL EXPENSES

Daily EXPENSE TRACKER

DATE	DESCRIPTION	CATEGORY	AMOUNT	CASH	CREDIT	DEBIT	NEED	WANT

TOTAL EXPENSES

Monthly Budget Worksheet

Month: _____   Year: _____

INCOME

- Income 1
- Income 2
- Other Income
- Total Income

DUE DATE	PAID	WHICH BILL	BUDGET	SPENT
		TOTAL		

SAVINGS

Starting Balance _____

Ending Balance _____

DEBT

Starting Balance _____

Ending Balance _____

GOALS

BY WHEN?	SAVING FOR WHAT?	MONTHLY GOAL	TOTAL NEEDED

ACTUALLY SAVED: _____

AMOUNT LEFT GOAL: _____

BY WHEN?	SAVING FOR WHAT?	MONTHLY GOAL	TOTAL NEEDED

ACTUALLY SAVED: _____

AMOUNT LEFT GOAL: _____

BY WHEN?	SAVING FOR WHAT?	MONTHLY GOAL	TOTAL NEEDED

ACTUALLY SAVED: _____

AMOUNT LEFT GOAL: _____

NOTES:

Daily EXPENSE TRACKER

DATE	DESCRIPTION	CATEGORY	AMOUNT	CASH	CREDIT	DEBIT	NEED	WANT

TOTAL EXPENSES

Daily EXPENSE TRACKER

DATE	DESCRIPTION	CATEGORY	AMOUNT	CASH	CREDIT	DEBIT	NEED	WANT

TOTAL EXPENSES

Daily EXPENSE TRACKER

DATE	DESCRIPTION	CATEGORY	AMOUNT	CASH	CREDIT	DEBIT	NEED	WANT

TOTAL EXPENSES

Monthly Budget Worksheet

Month : _____ Year : _____

INCOME

Income 1	Income 2
Other Income	Total Income

DUE DATE	PAID	WHICH BILL	BUDGET	SPENT
		TOTAL		

SAVINGS

Starting Balance _____

Ending Balance _____

DEBT

Starting Balance _____

Ending Balance _____

GOALS

BY WHEN?	SAVING FOR WHAT?	MONTHLY GOAL	TOTAL NEEDED

ACTUALLY SAVED: _____
AMOUNT LEFT GOAL: _____

BY WHEN?	SAVING FOR WHAT?	MONTHLY GOAL	TOTAL NEEDED

ACTUALLY SAVED: _____
AMOUNT LEFT GOAL: _____

BY WHEN?	SAVING FOR WHAT?	MONTHLY GOAL	TOTAL NEEDED

ACTUALLY SAVED: _____
AMOUNT LEFT GOAL: _____

NOTES:

Daily EXPENSE TRACKER

DATE	DESCRIPTION	CATEGORY	AMOUNT	CASH	CREDIT	DEBIT	NEED	WANT

TOTAL EXPENSES

Daily EXPENSE TRACKER

DATE	DESCRIPTION	CATEGORY	AMOUNT	CASH	CREDIT	DEBIT	NEED	WANT

TOTAL EXPENSES

Daily EXPENSE TRACKER

DATE	DESCRIPTION	CATEGORY	AMOUNT	CASH	CREDIT	DEBIT	NEED	WANT

TOTAL EXPENSES

Monthly Budget Worksheet

Month : _____   Year : _____

INCOME

Income 1	Income 2
Other Income	Total Income

SAVINGS

Starting Balance _____
Ending Balance _____

DEBT

Starting Balance _____
Ending Balance _____

DUE DATE	PAID	WHICH BILL	BUDGET	SPENT
		TOTAL		

GOALS

BY WHEN?	SAVING FOR WHAT?	MONTHLY GOAL	TOTAL NEEDED

ACTUALLY SAVED: _____
AMOUNT LEFT GOAL: _____

BY WHEN?	SAVING FOR WHAT?	MONTHLY GOAL	TOTAL NEEDED

ACTUALLY SAVED: _____
AMOUNT LEFT GOAL: _____

BY WHEN?	SAVING FOR WHAT?	MONTHLY GOAL	TOTAL NEEDED

ACTUALLY SAVED: _____
AMOUNT LEFT GOAL: _____

NOTES:

Daily EXPENSE TRACKER

DATE	DESCRIPTION	CATEGORY	AMOUNT	CASH	CREDIT	DEBIT	NEED	WANT

TOTAL EXPENSES

Daily EXPENSE TRACKER

DATE	DESCRIPTION	CATEGORY	AMOUNT	CASH	CREDIT	DEBIT	NEED	WANT

TOTAL EXPENSES

Daily EXPENSE TRACKER

DATE	DESCRIPTION	CATEGORY	AMOUNT	CASH	CREDIT	DEBIT	NEED	WANT

TOTAL EXPENSES

Monthly Budget Worksheet

Month : _____   Year : _____

INCOME

Income 1	Income 2
Other Income	Total Income

DUE DATE	PAID	WHICH BILL	BUDGET	SPENT
		TOTAL		

SAVINGS

Starting Balance _____

Ending Balance _____

DEBT

Starting Balance _____

Ending Balance _____

GOALS

BY WHEN?	SAVING FOR WHAT?	MONTHLY GOAL	TOTAL NEEDED

ACTUALLY SAVED: _____

AMOUNT LEFT GOAL: _____

BY WHEN?	SAVING FOR WHAT?	MONTHLY GOAL	TOTAL NEEDED

ACTUALLY SAVED: _____

AMOUNT LEFT GOAL: _____

BY WHEN?	SAVING FOR WHAT?	MONTHLY GOAL	TOTAL NEEDED

ACTUALLY SAVED: _____

AMOUNT LEFT GOAL: _____

NOTES:

Daily EXPENSE TRACKER

DATE	DESCRIPTION	CATEGORY	AMOUNT	CASH	CREDIT	DEBIT	NEED	WANT

TOTAL EXPENSES

Daily EXPENSE TRACKER

DATE	DESCRIPTION	CATEGORY	AMOUNT	CASH	CREDIT	DEBIT	NEED	WANT

TOTAL EXPENSES

Daily EXPENSE TRACKER

DATE	DESCRIPTION	CATEGORY	AMOUNT	CASH	CREDIT	DEBIT	NEED	WANT

TOTAL EXPENSES

NOTES

NOTES

NOTES

NOTES

NOTES

NOTES

NOTES

NOTES

NOTES

NOTES

Made in the USA
Monee, IL
23 January 2022